Oh Mind,
	Where
		Have
			You
				Gone
					Today?

By
	Hannah
		Blum

Oh, mind,
where have you gone today?
Perhaps you are tired,
run-down from racing,
no longer complacent.

But without you,
I don't feel like myself,
I am empty of thoughts,
lost.

Oh, mind,
where have you gone today?
I did not mean to push you away—
come back home
I want you to stay.

To my readers—

I love you
just as you are
for whatever you feel
high or low
messy or mindful
you are brilliant
and I'm honored.

THE FACETS OF MY MIND

MIND **MENDING** MADNESS

I have created a haven in my cocoon,
where I would like to remain
for some time,
to find myself,
sleep,
write,
not be a butterfly,
but to be present in what I feel.

I have disconnected from everyone
and I am
barely
hanging
onto
myself.

My emotions give me amnesia
and I will spend days,
maybe months,
even years,
begging to be seen,
to be reminded
of *who I am.*

I sat in the bath,
wrapped my arms around my body,
held her and asked,
"How do I learn to love you?"

When I isolate myself,
it feels like I'm missing out on life.
I fear that when I am no longer this way,
I will have missed out on too much.

If that is so, I will stay here,
watching life pass by
from my window.

Being alone feels
like home
and that's what
scares me the most.

The pain I've been suppressing
flows over the walls I've built.

Like a dam,
I hear it cracking.
Like a closet too full,
I hear it collapsing.

When I am numb
I stand in the shower.
I can think.
I can breathe.
The water does the
crying for me.

I do not know
what it means
to be present.

My mind lives
in other places
far away from
wherever it is

I am.

Unresolved trauma
haunts me like *ghosts.*

I. S I N K

I would come home each day,
and before I could say
one word to anyone,
I tiptoed to the bathroom,
closed the door,
turned the lock,
and the moment it clicked,
I felt safe.

I'd sit bare on the edge of the tub,
and pulled the knob up,
immersing myself in the water,
like a ship not strong enough
to carry its weight.

Everything was silent,
warm,
peaceful,
the opposite of what I felt.

When I could no longer
hold my breath,
I broke through the surface,
as if being reborn.

II. S I N K

I felt awake,
for a moment,
it all went away.

I laid my head back,
closed my eyes,
and waited for
the noise to begin
again.

More candles
and less people,
because I pushed them away.

Happy birthday.

Rocky roads
feel smooth
and untamed
waters *still.*

They call,
but we don't pick up.

They text,
but we don't respond.

They ask,
but we pretend we're fine,
turn off our phones,
and hide.

Why do we push them away?
Why is it hard to be honest?
To break down, not care.
I feel guilty,
ungrateful,
and confused.

Maybe you can relate
to the disconnect,
with ourselves,
with the world,
when they call,
and we don't pick up.

My words are stronger than me.
The picture I create,
more beautiful.
I sleep on a canvas
painting life
instead of living it.

I don't care,
and this is painful,
and foreign to me,
because I do care,
I know I do,
I'm just too tired to show it.

The pen holds my head
above water when I am
too weak to swim.

It's suppressing the urge to scream,
anxiety has me gasping
for air.

The guilt of having everything
but still feeling like nothing
weighs so heavily
I could *sink.*

Trauma pours the liquor
and softly whispers,

"Here.
This will make it
feel better."

There's nothing more intoxicating
than dancing till dawn,
sober as the *sunrise.*

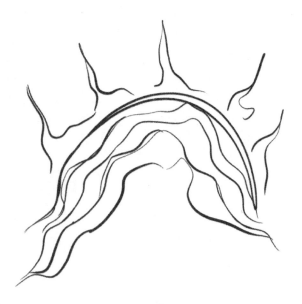

I don't want to look back on my life and reflect on all the experiences where I felt fulfillment, only to realize they were always in the presence of drugs and alcohol.

"Have I gone mad?"
—a question I ask
myself several times
a day.

My head feels disconnected
from my body,
like an object,
my mind so far from it.

Anxiety feels like
diving headfirst into
a dark ocean when you're
stepping over a puddle.

You are standing in the middle
of a frozen lake, one crack
and you'll be submerged
in the cold waters
of your pain.

The closeness of people
appear as hammers at bay,
and you must keep them away—

so, you isolate.

I C E O L A T I O N

My pillow absorbs
the wetness of my pain,
the screams,
a buoy that keeps me
from sinking into the bed.

I am always in a rush,
with a sense of urgency.
To be present is painful,
in stillness, darkness catches up.
I do not walk through life,

I run.

I feel nothing,
and somehow,
that is the worst feeling of all.

NUMB

I was born with an
addiction to emotion.
As much as I strive
to walk upon stable waters,
my mind always sails back
into the storm.

I curled up to my mother
as she lay on her bed,
at thirty-one years old,
I was a helpless child,
tears soaking into my cheeks.

I asked her the question,
the one that pained me,
"Are the extremes getting worse?"

She gently placed her hand
on my head, and replied,
"Yes, sweetheart."

I sighed with relief,
as if a ton had been lifted
off my shoulders,
to realize I was unwell
felt like freedom.

I turned my head towards her
and replied,
 "You're right.
It's time to get help."

I think about madness and
the people living with a mind
like mine. I think about what I have
witnessed and what I will spend
my life fighting for.

ACTIVIST

Revealing mental illness
is confessing to a crime
you never committed.
It's pleading guilty
when you are innocent.

Fall is my favorite season
favorite mood, it is peace
in the in-between,
something I struggle
to feel often.

A season without
extremes,

colors,
not too bright,
not too dark,

the air,
not too cold,
not too hot,

people,
not too covered,
not too bare.

A different feeling
accompanies this time of year,
sensitive and serene —
a perfect mix of the *in-between.*

Mental illness may be invisible,
but the people living with it
are
not.

My moods are not just
sadness and happiness,
they are different genres
and characters.

I want to rewrite the story of mental illness, a narrative that no longer casts those living with it as villains and everyone else as the victims. Igniting a fire within the soul of those who feel disempowered by their condition to be fearless in pursuing self-love and acceptance.

Bipolar feels like wearing
the Scarlet Letter—

a warning to others
'don't touch.
don't look.
don't love.'

> Yet, despite being
> branded as broken,
> this woman stands
> strong in all her Glory,
>
> a rose,
> adorned with thorns,
> her magic untouched.
>
> Do not let ignorance
> drive her into hiding,
> for this does not reflect
> her failings or wrongdoings,
> but yours.

It is there,
in the cemeteries
of abandoned asylums,
where you will see
graves marked with numbers,
headstones with no names.

BEDLAM HOSPITAL

I want to go sightseeing today.
I'll pay any fee to see
where they sleep,
chained below.
I desperately desire
to see madness up close.

I look forward to the day
when a vulnerable population
is not unfairly blamed for
the deranged and evil
actions of others.

They told me it was all in my head
but I know what I saw—
abuse happens behind
white walls.

I. WHITE COLUMNS

It was six p.m. when most of the staff left. I was sitting by the only window in the unit. I looked out to the parking lot as the staff approached their cars. Many wore smiles of relief, waving to each other. Some appeared to be gossiping, watching over their shoulders. One of the nurses opened her trunk and pulled out a black blouse, showing it to the others. Her demeanor made me wonder if she was going on a date.

Lastly, I saw my doctor swiftly get into his pristine car. I imagined that upon entering his home, one would be greeted by tall white columns.

I assumed their lives outside those white walls were perfect, their homes a place of happiness, but they were possibly trapped, too. Perhaps it was there, inside the hospital, that they felt free.

But they still went home. They slept in beds safely each night and showered without time restrictions and people standing nearby. They could kiss or call their loved ones to say goodnight.

II. WHITE COLUMNS

What I envied most was they had the freedom to decide when to turn the lights off. We had no other choice but to sleep in the dark.

Today, I decide when to turn the lights off.

THE PSYCHIATRIST

motivated by the ego,
and not the heart,
is poison to the
mental health system.

BEES AND HONEY

Upon entering the room, there it was, close enough to touch, Van Gogh's masterpiece, *Starry Night*, inspired by the view from his room at Saint-Paul-de-Mausole asylum. In the description box, mental illness is not considered taboo, but a significant piece of the master. Van Gogh lived with it, as do I.

I breathed in the blues and yellows, tranquility in chaos. However, I was interrupted by people pushing through to the front, cameras clicking, and questions being asked by eager visitors.

There they were, bewitched by the product of a brilliant and tortured mind. Society's admiration for the painting far exceeds its affection for the people who suffer just as he did, as many of us do.

Within the walls of that museum, our intensity and depth of emotions are embraced. Outside of it, we are treated more like burdens than beings and are no longer seen as brilliant but deranged.

All was quieted by the sound of my heels against the marble floor, walking away, watching them swarm madness like bees to a hive, desperate for *honey.*

She is a star,
radiating light that
dulls the brightness
of the moon,
an orphan to an icon,
beautiful blue-eyed muse.

But, even so,
applause could not
quiet the voices,
fame could not
fend off the monsters,
waking up in a nightmare,
costumed as a dream,

sweet Norma Jean.

I did not choose bipolar,
it chose me,
and is the only
mind I know.

I. GASLIGHT

I sit by my window and
see the light of the streetlamp
in the distance,
but he keeps telling me,

"It's off!
It's off!"

He believes I am crazy.
It puzzles me why he stays.

I see it clearly in the night—
the streetlamp is on,
I know it must be,
but he keeps telling me,

"It's off!
It's off!"

I will show him
he is wrong this time.

As I walk out
onto the broken sidewalk
I see a small yellow flower
blooming from the cracks.
I wish I could do the same.

II. G A S L I G H T

Reality is distorted.
I feel I've lost my mind,
my eyes, too cloudy to find it.

I stand alone in the dark.
He is right.
It is off.

but I saw the yellow flower...

Sometimes,
I wish my mental illness
would show up like a bruise,
and I could say to the world,

"I told you it was real.
Now, maybe you'll listen."

If you live with mental illness, don't wait for others to accept you. Put your energy towards loving yourself as you are without the validation of a society bleeding with judgment and ignorance.

IT IS SPRING,

a season of rebirth, and today,
I head into treatment for my mind
to rest for a while. Like the thawing earth,
I transition into a new cycle and mood.

On this road, I lost myself
somewhere a long time ago.
I am trying to find my way
back home to her.

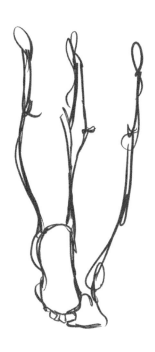

I fear this period of peace will end.
I only get a short time with it.
Not years.
Only seasons.

I thought my mind moved past it—
that with time
the pain would fade,
but my body remembers
all I have yet to face.

I want to come back to Earth. Grounded. I want to look at the stars without thinking beyond them. The anxiety about what has yet to arrive leaves me with self-doubt and insecurities. I do not want to keep living for tomorrow. I want to live for today. I am ready to be enough. The woman I should be is not as glorious as the woman I am in this moment. The same goes for you.

Come back to Earth.

I learned to love myself in isolation,
when the only person I could lean on
was myself.

She held me up.

I have spent so many years
hating myself, that loving myself
feels unfamiliar.

Now, I am ready.
You are too.

Sometimes, we think we are healing,
when really, we've just become good
at numbing the parts of ourselves that hurt.

COMMUNITY IS HEALING—

It is coping. Befriending those who struggle just as we do is the comforting hand that reminds us that the journey in pain is not traveled alone.

There is pain
in breaking,
but within it
lies freedom too.

Give yourself the same amount of love
that you freely give to others.
You deserve to bask in the warmth
of your affection, too.

It's a magical thing when you begin to value yourself. Those who do not appreciate you are less appealing; sadness is suddenly replaced by relief. They used to look much bigger and inferior. Now, they appear small, as if they have shrunk. You are no longer seeking validation. The time spent on someone who did not reciprocate your love is replaced with time loving yourself.

You are a mosaic,
a masterpiece
that doesn't exist without
being shattered along the way.

Love yourself whole,

    even when you feel
    less than half.

No matter who you are or where you come from, you possess wisdom ready to flow into the hearts and minds of others. Do not limit yourself. Allow your mind to wander like a curious child, eagerly seeking depth in places that may seem hollow on the surface.

TO THE DREAMER—

The dream isn't the hard part; it's believing in yourself enough to make it a reality. If you can break this barrier, those visions that once lived only in your mind will come to life. As you embark on this adventure, remember that dreams may not always unfold exactly as we imagine them. They demand time, adaptability, and an open mindset.

You will undoubtedly encounter days when quitting is tempting, self-doubt creeps in, and it feels like it's all over. When the winds blow fiercely and relentlessly, fear howls, "Turn around." But those howls will quiet with each step as you continue toward the realm where your dream is alive, waiting for you on the horizon.

Hiding in the word
smile is the word *lie.*
Be kind to those who
appear fine, for smiles
can hide the suffering inside.

BE OKAY

when you feel distant from the world. Be okay
with not having the energy to show up how you
want to on gloomy days. Walk in the rain without
an umbrella. Focus on the color, not the gray.
Mother Nature is unashamed of her inability to
produce sunlight every single day.

We should be too.

I looked at my pain and said,
"You're here, but instead of
crumbling like you want me to,
I will make something beautiful
out of you."

Just try
each day,
and if you fall again,
just try.

One step at a time,
and when you cannot step,
just rest.

Brighter places exist
outside of the dreams
you drift into.

You are
the sea,
the sky,
the sun,
the moon,
the stars.

You embody all
that's beautiful, and
raw in this world.

You don't have to carry their pain.
It was never yours to bear.
You deserve to feel light,
like a feather in the wind,
free again.

Do not quiet your imagination.
We live dull lives
without the magic
of our minds.

DISSOCIATING —

I feel myself disconnecting, so I close my eyes and imagine a garden growing within me. Roses bloom from my ribs, ivy weaves its way through me, and mystical willow trees ascend. I feel my roots, and the inner oasis whispers through the vines, "You're safe here."

(try this when you feel yourself detaching)

The Sun
was feeling
dull, worn,
not as bright,
not as warm.

For days, she
flooded the ground
with her tears.

Then the clouds cleared,
and there she saw below
pain birthed a flower
of her own.

You do love yourself.
If you didn't, you would
not fight so damn hard
to keep your head above water.

Define happiness without
anything material
or tangible.
Let it be as simple as
breathing in a new day.

Pain's journey,
our adventure's call.
Walking through storms
and toward rainbows, we go.

Embrace not only
the rainbow
but also, the storm
that set it free.

A CATERPILLAR

undergoes metamorphosis, emerging from a cocoon and entering a new stage. But even as it transforms, the light-hearted caterpillar that once crawled those crooked branches, like a locomotive without a destination, wiggling across curious humans, remains. Just in a different guise. Butterflies exude playfulness, innocence, and vibrancy. They retain that part of their former selves.

Come back to childlike wonder —
your *inner caterpillar.*

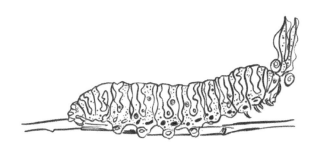

Self-love doesn't come from fixing yourself.
It comes from falling in love with the parts
of yourself, you've been trying to fix.

I sat beneath the waterfall in a hidden nook, the icy water caressing my bare skin and the sun gently warming my face. It felt like a baptism,
a moment of pure bliss amid emotional turmoil. I gazed at the rocks above, eroded yet beautiful. Their brokenness forged a path for the water's majestic descent toward freedom, evolving into something grander. The wisdom within those waters taught me that we, too, can carry our pain, letting it guide us toward openings of liberation, repeating the journey again and again.

YOSEMITE

You are a survivor,
thrown into an open ocean,
without a vest,
you taught yourself
to swim.

We cannot resurrect happiness by bringing back a time, a person, or a relationship where we once believed happiness existed. However, we do have the power to redesign it to be as, if not more, beautiful than before. No person or time owns your happiness, and trying to breathe life into the past keeps us gasping for air in the present.

Happiness is not a life
without sorrow.
Without sadness,
there is no room for joy.

I place my critical thoughts
on lily pads and watch them
float downstream,
the merciless lies
drifting away from me.

I know these thoughts
will return,
sooner than I'd like,

but so will the *lily pads.*

You are breaking
into becoming
again.

ECHOES OF **LOVE** AND LOSS

They see me,
but I do not feel seen.
Even when they lay
next to me,
I still feel alone.

You opened a place in my heart
I didn't know existed.
Now that you're gone
it echoes with emptiness,
and I do not know how
to make it full again.

I've always left before the sun rises
and they open their eyes.
It's selfish, foolish,

I know,

but my heart cannot bear
any more goodbyes
when I try to say hello,
and this is a tragic mindset,

I know,

but it's the truth,
that's why it's so easy to spill.

With men
sometimes
I feel like a drug—
a way to numb,
but the high never lasts.

I wish I could sleep heartbreak away,
and one day wake up
without this ache,
like Sleeping Beauty,
not waiting for a prince
but the kiss of peace.

I want them to stay, but
I don't know how to say it,
without feeling weak
and out of control.
I pretend I don't,
I show them the door,
the moment it shuts,
I fall to the floor,
and into my hands
I scream.

He is a Siren,
and knows what song
to sing to lure me
back in.

I swim towards him
again
and
again.

I didn't believe in vampires,
until I met him.
He made himself
full by emptying
me.

How did we end up here?
Lovers to strangers.

I didn't see it coming.
Like a train
without warning.

Now we are here.
A love story turned
to empty pages.

Manipulators light the flame
and blame you for the fire.

"I didn't mean to hurt you."
>Yes. You did.
>Told me to fall,
>held the net but
>didn't cast it.

"I'm sorry."
>No, you're not.
>If you were,
>you would not have
>continued stabbing
>the wound you created.

"I hope you forgive me."
>I don't.
>Not this time.

I've been burned so many times,
that when a man appears
I see *matches*
and g*asoline.*

She put her love on the line,
and he assumed it would remain—
it did for some time.

Then the wind picked up
and he saw the pieces
of her heart drifting away.

In a panic
he tried to catch them,

but it was too late.

In desperation
he shouted the words
she'd been yearning to hear
all along,

but it was too late.

She was ready to make
her heart whole again.

It didn't work out between us
because we were happy.

When we were together
the depression was quieter,
and we felt loved and accepted.

We loved each other deeply,
but it didn't work out
because we did not love ourselves.

Chasing people who do not love us back can feel more comfortable than being still with someone who does.

Love hard,
but be cautious with your heart.
Manipulators prey on the vulnerable
like wolves hunting *deer*.

Too many harsh words have been exchanged, and fights have left you empty. You have no other choice; it's over, not because you want it to be, but because it must be. It's painful and a relief. When the road behind you no longer exists, it is easier to walk forward.

I throw our love out
like a boomerang
with the hope
that it finds its way
back to me.

Our love began
in the clouds high above,
and although it seems romantic,
I wish we had a foundation,
grounding for growth,
because we've been falling
ever since, trying to find
a baseline.

IN LOVE,

I don't want to be the memory
hidden in boxes
stored away in the
back of a closet.

I want to be the memory
that ignites a smile,
a feeling of wholeness,
even for just a moment.

"Stay,"
she said.

"For how long?"
he asked.

"Is forever too long?"
she replied.

"Seems too short,"
he answered.

No matter how deep
into the woods I go,
I will always find my way
back to you.

Remember my smile,
capture it
like a photograph
that brings back memories
far beyond a single moment.
On days I am distant
remember my eyes,
soft and near,
full of light.

Find me like the stars
when darkness hovers.

My love,
I know your mind is far,
your pain too near,
but you are safe.
Come back to the
haven in my heart.

Them not loving you
does not make you unworthy.

Them not loving you
is their missed opportunity.

I. THERE SHE WAS

He walked into the house,
a storm had traveled through,
he felt it.
Walking into the bedroom,
windows open,
there she was,
the woman he loved,

sleeping soundly,
clutching the pillow
as a life vest,
puffs under her eyes
he knew she had been crying.

She beat herself down harder
than anyone else ever could,
fighting wars within,

sometimes, he wished it were him
who made her cry,
his mistakes he could fix,
he could not fix her,
he did not want to,
but she could never hate him—
she saved that for herself.

II. THERE SHE WAS

In her eyes,
she was nothing,
to him, she was everything
blanketed in vulnerability.

On faded days like this
he crawled into bed,
not one word said,

he waited for minutes,
sometimes hours,
to hear the rustling of the sheets,
and when he felt her touch
the clouds fell away,
not in the shadows alone,
she came home.

As the sun sank into the moon
he would sleep,
and so would she.

There she was,
the woman he loved.

No matter the day
or my mood,
regardless of what I say
or what I do,
I love you.

Whether distant
or far,
lost or found,
above or below,
I love you.

My mind wanders
but my heart never leaves.

I want him to know
he is loved,
in every moment,
with every pause.

When his eyes are afar,
I want to be home.

You have a unique way of loving that is unmatchable. I promise someone will stay to witness your magic.

You are not too much.
You've just been giving your heart
to those who love it too little.

When love begins to rob you of T I M E—Time away from the people who love you to be with someone whose love you question. Time spent on meaningless drama while missing out on meaningful experiences. Time away from your passion, and from loving yourself. Then, as hard as it is, it is T I M E to walk away.

I want to be loved for the raw,
unedited version of myself.
A love that wears no filters.

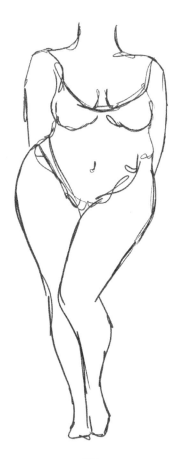

Love lives far beyond
our eyes, for if it did not,
why is it that when coffins close
people still cry?

I want to drop my guard,
open my heart.
I want to be soft, warm,
I just want to melt in his arms.

I met him
in my dream
last night.

I sat on the floor.
Eyes dark from no sleep.

I did not have to say a word.
I felt safe.

For the first time in years,
I slept.

I can no longer stand on the sand
watching your love
come in and out
like the tide.

I'm ready to swim.

He woke up the parts of me
that had been asleep for so long.

V O W S

I've never really thought about my wedding. I am not against marriage, but the fear of getting too attached to the idea of forever scares me. But if I could daydream about it...

I imagine only two will attend, me and him, he and I. Maybe in a courthouse or by the sea or an empty church. We would shut the world out, trace each other's mouths, and picture our lives together. Sharing vows that would remain in the space between us.

It will not only be a day to celebrate a beginning in love, but also a day to commemorate the ending of my war with it.

Big weddings are beautiful, too, and maybe I will have a huge parade, and I will look back and laugh, but for now, I imagine my wedding day, only two will attend,

he and I,
me and him.

She looked to the sunset and said,
"I didn't know God could create
something so beautiful."

He looked at her,
"Neither did I."

SENSUAL **AWAKE**NING

SENSUALITY

goes far beyond the physical realm. It nurtures playfulness, empowerment, connection, and imagination. Instead of superficial imagery, it invites us into a world of fantasies, where we embody the essence of femininity at its most exquisite.

I am being baptized by the
hands of a newfound sensuality.
One where my body is sacred,
no longer an object, or
a platform for abuse,
but seen for what it truly is—
beautiful.

He wanted something sweet.
So I led him down,
and below my waist,
he sunk.
I whispered,

"Here's something sweet.
Now eat."

Embrace your sensuality. Embody your femininity unapologetically. You can express your desires without feeling perverse and assert boundaries without feeling like a prude. Boundaries are your birthright; establish them and honor yourself.

I thought if I gave them my body
they would give me their heart.
Oh, how wrong I was.

S * x
is not supposed to feel
like an audition.
But it does.

S * x
is not supposed to feel
like a competition.
But it does.

S * x
is supposed to feel
comfortable,
respectful,
fun,
intimate,
uninhibited.

Kiss me.
Let me feel what you
are too afraid to say.

You taste familiar.
Your tongue,
its flavor.
I've been here before,
in Euphoria.

I felt you coming.
Must be
déjà vu.

Come to bed, my love.
Let's disappear into the night.
Fade in between the sheets.
Bond.
Become one.

Touch me
from the inside *out.*

I whisper across his neck,
down his chest.
He is my muse
and tonight
I am his oracle.

His lips travel
my stretchmarks
          like a trail.

Over the dips
of my hips
          like hills.

Unearthing my curves,
he unlocks my legs
          and explores.

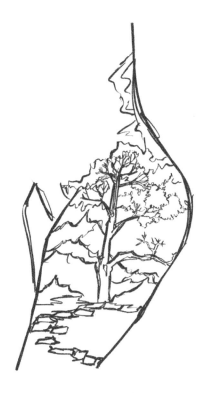

"Meditate for me."

His voice anchored my mind
in the present.
Eyes closed,
thoughts adrift,
he eased in every inch,
making love
to every crevice inside of me.

He whispered,

 "Breathe.
Hold it for three."

I am polite.
Well mannered.
A fine hostess.

When they enter
my bedroom,
I always ask,

"Are you hungry?"

The way his mouth dances
between my thighs
leaves me mesmerized.

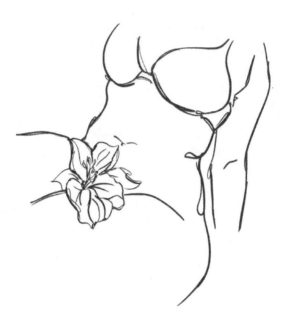

He plays my body
like Mozart
does
the
keys.

He was my ocean—
he came in and out of me
like the tide and went
deeper and deeper
each and every time.

Dive deep into your fantasy.
Close your eyes
and let your mind drift.
Your body is the piano.
Your fingers play the keys.

Sing.

I imagine myself floating in a sheer dress at night, my body lit by the stars, my heart touched by the grandness of the sky and the vastness of the sea. I observe myself gliding across the surface, unedited. Close your eyes and wander to this place. Let your anxiety fade into the waves. Set yourself free and *float.*

EMPOW**HER**ED

A woman
who is a stranger
is still a sister.

My mother is magic.
She is unforgettable.
The greatest poet
I have ever known.
She does not write about life—
she lives every moment of it.

A woman can be so many different things
all at once, multidimensional,
a shapeshifter.

It is in her blood.

Her heart is a hive,
pure honey.
Not even the sun
can match her warmth,
nor can the stars reflect
her light.

It is an act of defiance
for a woman to love herself
in a society that sets her up
to hate herself.

Beauty does not fade,
it transitions,
marking a timeless era,
unfolding like a journey
through the seasons.

TO MY SISTERS—

we will reach even greater heights when we embrace one another as companions rather than competitors.

To remain young
is to die young.

Those who left too soon
would bask in old age,
rejoice in the wisdom gained,
embrace every line,
every wrinkle,
trails that tell tales
of a long life.

Do not let vanity
blind you to the beauty
of aging, for the alternative
is far more tragic.

I want to be beautiful,
like a book.
Classic, everlasting,
measured by what
is written beneath
the exterior.

You do not lower the bar
for any man.
You raise the bar
and challenge him to rise.

I am not naive to bad men,
nor am I blind to good men.

Stretchmarks are not flaws.
They are a testament to the beauty
of a body that evolves and transforms.

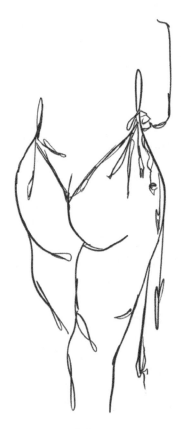

I see motherhood on the horizon.
I see it coming towards me,
not today,
not tomorrow,
not a year from now,

but I see it on the horizon,
motherhood is closer to me.

No matter the action or wrongdoing,
the bad men win when they rob us
of our ability to see the good.

She *trans*itioned into a butterfly
with wings more familiar
and connected.

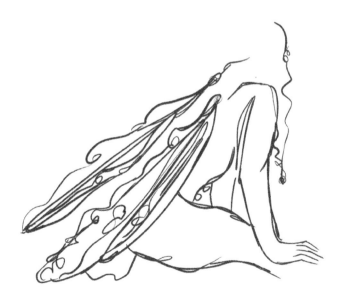

Original sin follows women,
and we spend our lives
in repentance.

Be a good girl
or *be quiet.*

Eve did not break God's law.
She broke Man's law.

In the Garden of Eden,
God witnessed the
rebellious soul
of a woman.

Scripture taught me
to love God out of fear—
like a woman saying
"I love you" to her
abusive husband.

Scripture taught me
to obey a man
like a dog does
their master.

How can I abide
by a book that reads
She is lesser than Him?

For God does not
shame women.

Yet, He appears more
as a manipulator than
a loving spirit in the words
of the Scripture.

It is not Godly
or righteous
to rob a woman
of her freedom to choose.

Her body
is not
His choice.

BRIDGING **DIVIDES**

From the window of our kitchens
within reaching distance
no longer a friend —
we see the enemy.

No more conversations
between fences
but silence held
between barricades.

AMERICAN NEIGHBORS TODAY

If my words
can build bridges
between people,
wide and narrow,
they have done
justice.

I walk from the streets of DC to tobacco fields, traveling urban and rural terrains, mending wounds, and bridging gaps in hopes of birthing change.

Desperate for attention
the sound of applause
rings louder
in the Politician's ear
than the cries of the people.

The invisible farmer
is told he is seen by politicians
who have never walked
nor watered
his fields.

I eagerly await the day
when front yards are not
stages for propaganda,
and gatherings no longer
venues for debates.

When we uncover
common ground
and unity in their place.

Once a person living in the shadows is finally seen, they'll traverse any path to maintain that visibility. The sensation of being overlooked ignites their anger.

AMERICAN GIRL

I dance to the melody
sung by Sweet Liberty,
resonating with hope
and boundless possibility.

I see the beauty and potential
of my country, and I will never
give up on the people.

I see pollution in the air.
Must be the Politician—
Speaking jargon.
Spewing lies.

A CLIMATE CRISIS

If only we listened without the intent to debate, to fulfill our egos and agendas, we would be in a much better place.

Beneath the canopy of the sky,
I see it swaying in the wind,
three different hues,

red,
white,
and
blue,

moving
as one.

WASHINGTON MONUMENT D.C.

Conflict will always be present
and change, always possible.

HUMAN TAPESTRY

I do not see strangers,
I see people I have yet
to explore.

Let curiosity be your life's compass, guiding you to discover the threads that connect us all. When you reach outwards, you will experience a profound sense of wholeness, purpose, and unity with others.

EXPLORE HUMANITY

Smiles as they pull up,
quiet whimpers as they leave.
It is there where planes fly,
that you will see the cycle
of *love* and *grief.*

You have the right
to define your spirituality.

Your relationship with God
or a higher power is yours to create.

You can believe
in the Bible or not.

You can believe
in the Universe or not.

You can live a life absent
of belief or not.

Our differences
should not create wars —
they should be embraced.

POLLUTED HEARTS

I see a homeless man sleeping on the sidewalk, covered in filth, and one block ahead, members of a climate organization distributing eco-friendly tote bags with the text *Save Our Planet*. A sadness washes over me because as long as this homeless man lies here forgotten, the Earth will wither due to our collective disregard for human suffering. It's right there before us, but we pass by with casual detachment. Humans need cleansing, guided not by the ego but by the heart. Empathy is the lifeline of Mother Earth; without it, she will struggle to hold us up.

Why do we wait for
the funeral to show
compassion and
send flowers?

Why do we wait for
their eyes to close
to make them feel seen?

Why do we show up
in the wake of suicide
but not while alive?

W H Y ?

There is a place I go, and
there stands a peculiar tree,

branches covered in thorns,
long spines intertwined,
a mystery of a tree,

kind of like you,
kind of like me.

As people walk by,
curiosity uncovers their eyes,
opens their mind,
and they see beauty in what
appears to be different
from the rest of nature
which seamlessly blends.

B A L B O A   P A R K

I love the memories with friends that are not documented in photos or videos — moments only captured by the heart and mind.

When a man cries
he does not see his strength —
eyes glisten with vulnerability,
he is Glorious.

Envy has the power
to turn beautiful people
into bitter souls.

Catch it
the moment you feel it,
hold it with love,
embrace the glory of
other humans reaching
golden places,

just as you do,
and just as *you will.*

I. BEARING WITNESS TO LOVE

It was after the funeral. I walked onto the porch and stood alongside the father, mourning the death of his twenty-year-old son. As we spoke, he mentioned that he had not informed his mother about her grandson's death. 'She has dementia,' he explained. There was a moment of silence. Then, he turned to me with glossy eyes,

"How lucky she is.
To *forget.*"

Suddenly, the idea of not remembering seemed like a dream. Losing all comprehension of what is happening around you was more of an escape from suffering than a debilitating condition.

But then his foggy eyes began to clear as he looked through the open doors into the living room, where photos of his son graced every corner, portraying a compelling soul, wise beyond his years, whose very presence served as inspiration.

A smile lifted on his face.

II. BEARING WITNESS TO LOVE

Even when forgetfulness was so tempting, he would never choose it because that would mean losing memories of his son. He would bear the deepest pain every day to remain in a reality where he could continue loving his child.

I witnessed love at its most unrefined, like sap flowing from the heart of a maple tree.

It dawned on me—

Love is not hard.

Life is.

If beauty, money, fame, social media *likes,* and follows bring happiness and fullness, why does it seem that most people with those things seem sad and empty?

Maybe we got it wrong.

Human laughter is the song
that soothes the soul,
fills the heart,
a flicker of light
in the darkest rooms.

ONCE IN AWHILE,

take off your headphones, close your eyes, and listen to the symphony. The sirens and horns, the subtle whistling of wind gusts, the rustling of leaves or cicadas singing in Summer, the footsteps of passersby, and the distant hum of conversations.

It's life's most beautiful ballad.

The wisest person
is the one who
listens the most.

I see the moon tonight
and wonder if she touched
the eyes of the warrior people.

Or was the sky too gray
and flooded with the haze
of bombs built for bloodshed?

This moon has witnessed
the burden of evil and the power
of the human spirit all before
circling the earth to me.

He was no veteran,
he had yet to retire
from the war that ended
decades ago.

Still under the monsoon,
in elephant grass fields,
waiting to come home—

he left Vietnam,
but Vietnam never left him.

Before bedtime the boy
asked his mother,
"Where do soldiers sleep?"

And she replied,

"Some sleep in barracks on bunks,
others on campgrounds in faraway places,
and many sleep on beds in their homes.
But many soldiers sleep in tents,
not in deserts or mountain ranges,
but on sidewalks and streets."

They asked her
"How do you write."

She replied
"I listen."

IN THE DISTANCE,

a well-groomed dog sniffs at the homeless man's shoes and jumps into his worn blanket. The owner jerks the leash with a disgusted look across her face as if her pooch were sniffing poison, but this man is no toxin; he is human. Open your eyes to people we cast aside like garbage.

The Bigot
is the hunter of people.
Birthed from fear, he lives
in the shadows of evil.

He asked me
"What is your favorite
sound?"

I answered with the first
sound that came to mind —

 "The sound of birds
chirping at the crack of dawn
right before the sun greets us
with *'hello.'*"

My pockets are empty
but my life is full.

Homey the Hummingbird
is the name I gave him
and each morning
I wake up to his song.

Wiggling his feathers,
warmed by the sun,
looking for something,
or someone,
maybe searching
for a different place,
but he always comes back
to the tree outside my window.

He must feel safe here,
as do I, and one day
he will fly away
as will I.

I light another one,
and hear fire
kissing tobacco,
crackling,
pouring over my lips
like a deep fog creeping in.

I. BOATS PASSING BY

A man was lost in the ocean,
struggling to keep his head
above water, close to
drowning.

Then, the waters began rocking,
a boat was approaching,
a woman was waving.

With hope in his eyes,
he reached out his hand,

but to his surprise
she was not reaching back,
instead, the woman looked
disappointingly at him and yelled,

"You're not drowning,
it's all in your head,
swim to the shore instead."

Then she sailed away.

The man did what she said,
he tried to quiet the thoughts.
There were moments of relief,
then he felt weak and
began to struggle again.

II. BOATS PASSING BY

Then, the waters began rocking,
another boat was approaching,
a man was waving.

With hope in his eyes,
he reached out his hand,

but saw this man
was not reaching back.
Instead, the man who called
himself a *guru* yelled,

"You're not drowning,
it's an illusion, you see.
Strengthen your body,
gaze at the sky, manifest
your desire to survive."

Then he sailed away.

The man did what the *guru* advised,
exercising his mind,
striving to survive,
at times, he felt strong,
but it did not last for long,
and he began to struggle again.

III. BOATS PASSING BY

Boats kept coming,
one after the other.

Some told him to pray,
God would save him that day.
People waving, voicing their
theories on healing.

Not one person listened,
or asked questions,

their egos steered the boat,
their hearts just along for the ride.

The pain of being misunderstood,
and feeling invisible
became too much to bear.

He was ready to sink.

Then, the waters began rocking,
another boat was approaching,
a woman was steering,

but he was too tired,
and did not reach out
his hand this time.

IV. BOATS PASSING BY

To his surprise, the woman
was not waving
or yelling.

Empathy exuded from her eyes
like a guiding light.

She dove into the water,
igniting ripples of hope,
swam to him, and
reached out her hand,

breathlessly, she said,

"I see you."

His pain was as real
as his strength,
through the suffering
he kept swimming,
and made his way to shore.

He turned and waved
to the *boats passing by.*

THANK YOU

for coming along on this journey. You will write many more chapters. Fill them with truth, exploration, love, and madness. Do not let yourself be limited by anything. Bloom in every direction.

SOURCES & INSPIRATION

I want to credit sources and publications that offered insights that inspired some of the poems and essays.

Hawthorne, Nathaniel. *The Scarlet Letter*. 1850.

The poem on page 47 was inspired by the book *Bedlam: An Intimate Journey into America's Mental Health Crisis* by Rosenberg, Kenneth Paul.

The poem on page 155 that refers to 'Mozart' is metaphorical and does not pertain to the composer Wolfgang Amadeus Mozart.

Made in the USA
Las Vegas, NV
13 September 2024